Mastering Affiliate Marketing

"A Comprehensive Guide to Building a Lucrative Online Business"

Patrick Odega

Dedication

To all the dedicated affiliate marketers out there, who work tirelessly to promote products and services they believe in, who constantly experiment and innovate to find new ways to drive traffic and increase conversions, who are always learning and adapting to changes in the industry, and who understand that success in affiliate marketing is not an overnight phenomenon, but the result of consistent effort and perseverance. This dedication is for you.

Table Of Contents

Chapter 1

Introduction to Affiliate Marketing

Affiliate marketing is a performance-based marketing strategy in which an affiliate promotes a merchant's product or service and earns a commission for each successful sale, lead, or action. The affiliate promotes the product or service to their audience through various marketing channels such as their website, social media, email marketing, or paid advertising.

Affiliate marketing is a lucrative business model because it allows affiliates to earn passive income by promoting products or services that they believe in, without having to create or own the product themselves. It also provides merchants with a cost-effective way to reach a wider audience and increase sales.

There are different types of affiliate marketing, including:

1. **Pay-per-sale (PPS)** – In this model, the affiliate earns a commission for each sale made through their unique affiliate link.
2. **Pay-per-click (PPC)** – In this model, the affiliate earns a commission for each click made through their affiliate link, regardless of whether a sale is made.

3. **Pay-per-lead (PPL)** – In this model, the affiliate earns a commission for each lead or sign-up generated through their affiliate link.
4. **Pay-per-call (PPC)** – In this model, the affiliate earns a commission for each phone call made by a referred customer to the merchant's phone number.

To become a successful affiliate marketer, it's important to choose the right niche and products to promote, create high-quality content that resonates with your audience, and drive targeted traffic to your website or landing pages.

It's also important to understand the different commission structures and affiliate programs available in your niche, and to build strong relationships with affiliate partners and merchants.

Another key aspect of successful affiliate marketing is to stay compliant with FTC guidelines and maintain ethical and transparent marketing practices.

While affiliate marketing can be a highly lucrative business model, it requires consistent effort and dedication to achieve success. However, with the right mindset, strategies, and tools, anyone can master affiliate marketing and build a profitable online business

Chapter 2

Finding Profitable Niches and Products

Choosing the right niche for affiliate marketing is crucial to the success of your business.

Here are some tips for choosing a profitable niche:

1. **Identify your interests and passions -** Start by choosing a niche that you are passionate about or have some level of interest in. This will make it easier for you to create content and stay motivated in the long run.
2. **Research market demand -** Look for niches that have a high demand but relatively low competition. You can use keyword research tools like Google Keyword Planner, SEMrush, or Ahrefs to determine the search volume and competition of different niches.
3. **Consider profitability -** Choose a niche that has high-profit potential. Look for products or services that have a high commission rate and a proven track record of generating sales.

Once you have chosen your niche, the next step is to research profitable affiliate products and services.

Here are some tips for conducting research:

1. **Look for established and reputable merchants -** Choose merchants who have a good reputation in the industry and offer high-quality products or services.
2. **Check commission rates and payment terms -** Look for merchants who offer a high commission rate and have a reliable payment system in place.
3. **Consider the product demand and customer satisfaction -** Look for products or services that have a high demand and positive customer reviews.

After identifying profitable products, it's essential to analyze the competition in your niche.

Here are some tips for analyzing competition:

1. **Identify your competitors -** Look for websites or businesses that are targeting the same audience as you.
2. **Analyze their website and content -** Analyze their website design, content, keywords, and backlinks to determine their strengths and weaknesses.
3. **Look for gaps and opportunities -** Look for areas where your competitors are not meeting the needs of their audience and find ways to fill those gaps.

By choosing a profitable niche, researching profitable products, and analyzing the competition, you can set yourself up for success in affiliate marketing.

Chapter 3

Building Your Affiliate Marketing Website

reating a website is an essential step in building your affiliate marketing business.

Here are some tips for creating a website:

1. **Choose a domain name and hosting provider -** Choose a domain name that is relevant to your niche and easy to remember. There are many hosting providers to choose from, but it's important to choose one that is reliable, secure, and offers good customer support.

2. **Select a platform -** There are many website builders and content management systems available, such as WordPress, Wix, or Squarespace. Choose a platform that meets your needs and skill level.

3. **Create quality content -** Your website content should be high-quality, informative, and engaging. Use a mix of text, images, and videos to keep your audience interested.

4. **Optimize for search engines -** Use keyword research to optimize your content for search engines. This will help improve your website's visibility and drive more traffic to your site.

5. **Design an attractive and user-friendly website -** Your website design should be

attractive, easy to navigate, and user-friendly. Use a responsive design that looks great on all devices, and make sure your website loads quickly to avoid losing visitors.

6. **Include call-to-actions** - Include call-to-actions on your website to encourage visitors to take action. This could be signing up for a newsletter, downloading a guide, or making a purchase.
7. **Build a mailing list** - Include a mailing list signup form on your website to build a list of subscribers. This is an effective way to keep in touch with your audience and promote your affiliate products.
8. **Incorporate affiliate links** - Include affiliate links throughout your website in a way that is natural and non-intrusive. Avoid using too many affiliate links, as this can come across as spammy and may turn off your audience.
9. **Use analytics** - Use analytics tools like Google Analytics to track your website traffic and monitor the performance of your affiliate links. This will help you make informed decisions about your website and optimize your affiliate marketing strategy.
10. **Stay up-to-date** - Keep your website up-to-date with fresh content and new affiliate products. This will help you stay relevant in

your niche and maintain the interest of your
audience.

By following these tips, you can create a website that
is optimized for affiliate marketing and designed to
attract and retain visitors. Remember, your website is
the foundation of your affiliate marketing business, so
it's essential to invest time and effort into building a
high-quality website.

Chapter 4

Creating High-Quality Content

High-quality content is crucial for the success of your affiliate marketing business.

Here are some tips for creating content that resonates with your target audience:

1. **Understand your audience** - Identify your target audience and create content that meets their needs and interests. This could include tutorials, how-to guides, or product reviews.
2. **Use compelling headlines** - Use headlines that grab the attention of your audience and make them want to read more.
3. **Provide value** - Create content that provides value to your audience. This could include insights, tips, or advice that helps them solve a problem or achieve a goal.
4. **Be authentic** - Write in a natural and authentic voice that resonates with your audience. Avoid using salesy or promotional language, as this can turn off your audience.
5. **Incorporate visuals** - Use images and videos to make your content more engaging and visually appealing.
6. **Include calls-to-action** - Include calls-to-action in your content to encourage your audience to take action. This could be signing up for a newsletter or making a purchase.

7. **Write product reviews and recommendations** - Write honest and detailed product reviews that provide value to your audience. Share your personal experiences and opinions to help your audience make informed purchasing decisions.

 Creating high-quality content that resonates with your target audience, you can build trust and authority in your niche, attract more visitors to your website, and increase your affiliate sales. Remember to stay focused on providing value and serving your audience, and the results will follow.

Chapter 5

Driving Traffic to Your Website

Once you have created high-quality content and built an affiliate marketing website, the next step is to drive traffic to your website.

Here are some strategies for driving traffic to your website:

1. **Search engine optimization (SEO) -** Optimize your website for search engines by using relevant keywords, meta descriptions, and optimizing your content for search engines. This will help your website rank higher in search engine results pages (SERPs).

2. **Social media marketing -** Use social media platforms to promote your content and drive traffic to your website. Share your content on platforms like Facebook, Twitter, and LinkedIn, and engage with your audience to build a following.

3. **Paid advertising -** Use paid advertising platforms like Google Ads and Facebook Ads to drive targeted traffic to your website. This can be a great way to get your content in front of a larger audience and increase your affiliate sales.

4. **Guest posting -** Write guest posts for other websites in your niche, and include a link back

to your website. This can help drive traffic to your website and increase your visibility in your niche.

5. **Email marketing** - Build an email list and use email marketing to drive traffic to your website. Send out regular newsletters and promotional emails that include links back to your website.

By using these strategies, you can drive targeted traffic to your website and increase your affiliate sales. Remember to focus on providing value to your audience and building relationships, and the results will follow.

Chapter 6

Maximizing Your Affiliate Revenue

nce you have built a website, created high-quality content, and started driving traffic to your website, the next step is to maximize your affiliate revenue.

Here are some strategies for maximizing your affiliate revenue:

1. **Understand different affiliate programs and commission structures** - Research different affiliate programs and

2.
   commission structures to find the ones that offer the best
   commission rates and are most relevant to your audience.

3. **Track your affiliate links and conversions** - Use affiliate tracking software to track your affiliate links and conversions. This will help you identify which affiliate programs and products are generating the most revenue for your business.

4. **Build relationships with affiliate partners** - Build relationships with your affiliate partners by providing value, communicating regularly, and offering feedback. This can help you secure exclusive deals and higher commission rates.
5. **Use A/B testing** - Use A/B testing to optimize your website and improve your affiliate conversions. Test different landing pages, headlines, and calls-to-action to see what works best for your audience.
6. **Offer bonuses and incentives -** Offer bonuses and incentives to your audience to encourage them to purchase products through your affiliate links. This could include exclusive content, discounts, or free products.

Implementing these strategies, you can maximize your affiliate revenue and build a sustainable and profitable affiliate marketing business. Remember to focus on building relationships, providing value to your audience, and continually testing and optimizing your website and content.

Chapter 7

Scaling Your Affiliate Marketing Business

Once you have established a profitable affiliate marketing business, the next step is to scale your business to achieve even greater success. **Here are some strategies for scaling your affiliate marketing business:**

1. **Expand your product range** - Look for new affiliate products and services that are relevant to your niche and audience. This can help you increase your revenue and grow your business.

2. **Outsource tasks and hire a team -** As your business grows, you may need to outsource certain tasks or hire a team to help you manage your affiliate marketing business. This could include hiring a virtual assistant, a writer, or a social media manager.

3. **Expand to new niches and markets** - Consider expanding your business to new niches and markets to reach a broader audience. This could involve creating new websites or building new social media channels.

4. **Invest in paid advertising** - Consider investing in paid advertising to drive more traffic to your website and increase your revenue. This could include running ads on social media platforms, using Google Ads, or partnering with other websites in your niche.

5. **Create new revenue streams** - Look for opportunities to create new revenue streams, such as selling digital products or offering coaching services to your audience.

Using these strategies, you can scale your affiliate marketing business and achieve even greater success. Remember to stay focused on your goals, continue to provide value to your audience, and always be looking for new opportunities to grow your business.

Chapter 8

Avoiding Common Affiliate Marketing Mistakes

While affiliate marketing can be a highly profitable business model, there are also some common mistakes that many affiliate marketers make. Here are some of the most common mistakes and how to avoid them:

- **Choosing the wrong products** - One of the biggest mistakes affiliate marketers make is choosing the wrong products to promote. Make sure to research the products and services thoroughly before promoting them to your audience. Only promote products that are high quality, relevant to your niche, and have a good reputation.

- **Not disclosing affiliate relationships** - It is important to disclose your affiliate relationships to your audience. This means letting them know that you will earn a commission if they make a purchase through your affiliate link. Failure to disclose this information can damage your reputation and violate legal requirements.

- **Focusing solely on promoting products** - While promoting products is the main focus of affiliate marketing, it is important to also focus on providing value to your audience. Create high-quality content that provides value to your audience and helps them solve problems.

- **Not tracking your results -** It is important to track your results and analyze your data to see what is working and what is not. Use tracking software to track your clicks, conversions, and revenue. This will help you optimize your website and content for maximum performance.
- **Giving up too soon -** Building a successful affiliate marketing business takes time and effort. Many affiliate marketers give up too soon, before they see the results of their efforts. Stay committed, stay consistent, and keep working hard to build your business.

By avoiding these common mistakes, you can build a successful and profitable affiliate marketing business. Remember to focus on providing value to your audience, choosing high-quality products, and tracking your results to optimize your performance.

Chapter 9
Conclusion and Next Steps

In conclusion, affiliate marketing is a lucrative business model that can generate passive income for those who are willing to put in the time and effort to build a successful business. By choosing a profitable niche, creating high-quality content, driving traffic to your website, and maximizing your affiliate revenue, you can build a profitable affiliate marketing business.

To take your affiliate marketing business to the next level, consider implementing the following actionable steps:

- Continuously research your niche and target audience to stay up-to-date on trends and changes in your industry.

- Focus on creating high-quality content that provides value to your audience.

- Optimize your website and content for search engines to drive more traffic to your site.

- Build relationships with affiliate partners and continuously look for new products and services to promote.

- Track your results and use data to optimize your performance and improve your business.

As you continue to build your affiliate marketing business, there are many resources and tools available to help you succeed. These include affiliate marketing networks, tracking software, and educational resources such as blogs, courses, and webinars.

Remember, building a successful affiliate marketing business takes time, effort, and dedication. Stay committed, stay focused on providing value to your audience, and never stop learning and growing as an affiliate marketer. With persistence and hard work, you can build a profitable and sustainable affiliate marketing business.

www.ingramcontent.com/pod-product-compliance
Lightning Source LLC
Chambersburg PA
CBHW070752220526

45467CB00018B/2123